ARK PIZARRO

ADVANCING POSSIBILITIES

ESSENTIAL ENTREPRENEURSHIP TRAINING TO TRANSFORM YOUR THINKING AND START GROWING A SUCCESSFUL BUSINESS ONLINE

To my beautiful wife Gilsa, who has been with me through the highs and lows. I love you, and thank you for building this wonderful life with me.

To my kids, Alex, Marcos, Andy, and Christine, you are my greatest achievement and the reason I strive. I love each one of you more than you know.

To my parents, Amy and Joe, for always being there for me and teaching me the importance of family, faith, and hard work.
I love you.

A journey of a thousand miles must begin with a single step.

- LAO TZU

Contents

ADVANCING POSSIBILITIES

Preface

Life is a journey, and the way I got to where I am today is by no means conventional. In 2008, I had two great jobs, an easy schedule, and I was making good money. My bosses loved me, and without a doubt, I was on my way up. I was also preparing to complete my medical licensing exam and focus on my career as a physician.

But there was one big problem. My wife and our three boys were overseas in her country, the Dominican Republic. Her immigration papers were taking forever to be processed. I later learned that her documents had apparently been "lost" in the system. So, after spending too many sleepless nights staring at the ceiling, I decided I'd rather be a full-time husband and dad than a doctor. I resigned from my positions, packed my bags, and headed to the Caribbean to be with my family.

A physician's salary in the Dominican Republic pales compared to the United States, so I decided practicing medicine was not an option. On the other hand, running my own business sounded a lot more attractive and doable. I had been a partner in a small marketing business in the past, and my taste for business had never waned. I always stayed on top of the latest business books and magazines. So, how hard could it be, right?

My original plan was to create an internet startup. But I ran into so many hurdles (the greatest of these being my mindset) that I decided to shift my focus elsewhere. I started learning everything I could about building an online business. Eventually, I became pretty good at developing WordPress websites. Though a web designer I'm not, working with websites helped me discover internet marketing. And just like that... my second career was born!

My appetite for learning all there was to know about internet marketing grew exponentially. But course after course and eBook after eBook left me with a sour taste in my mouth. The terminology and concepts were poorly taught, and that made learning slow and frustrating. The majority of marketers didn't provide sufficient value to help me create a real solution. I always felt like they were holding something back.

To make a bad situation worse, the big-name "gurus" just weren't within my reach financially. Instead, I studied their product launch videos and scoured Google and YouTube to get a better handle on what they were teaching. My hat goes off to Jeff Johnson because, for me, he was the first guru to provide excellent content on YouTube.

Eben Pagan was another one who truly raised the bar in terms of product launch content by "moving the free line," as he used to say. In other words, he was giving away gold nuggets while most were only giving away chicken nuggets. Keep in mind these were the early days of YouTube; it has changed a great deal since then. None the less I want to give a big thanks to Jeff and Eben!

I studied for months (now years), and it got to the point where my friends and family could no longer relate to my conversations. It was like I was talking in code all the time, SEO, PPC, CTR, LTV, ROI, and they were wondering what all these government agencies were that they'd never heard of before. I hate to admit it, but my intense focus on the business aspect of my life alienated many.

If you only learn one thing from me, let it be that above all else, you should always put your spouse and children first. We (ambitious types) can become obsessed with success and lose sight of 'whom' and 'what' really matters. Making lots of money is great, and you have your entire life to work at that, but you only get one chance to watch your kids grow up.

This whole learning without earning process took its toll until I was finally ready to throw in the towel and never look back at doing business online again. One morning I sat down in front of my computer and said to myself, "Ark, just give it one last shot."

So, I mapped out what I wanted to achieve in my business. This was big, because how can you get to where you're going if you don't know where you want to go? Then, I stumbled upon a marketer named James Schramko, whose teachings really resonated with me. I saw that James was big on systems and that he was where I wanted to be. Now, I was sure that I was on to something.

I tested my own system, and it worked. I started making money! I taught my system to a few close friends, and they also succeeded in making money. Those were some exciting times; seeing our bank accounts grow while we slept was amazing!

I shared these strategies with a couple of local business owners I knew, and guess what happened? It worked for them too! That's when I knew I had to share this with the millions of people out there who continually struggle to get by. Those same people who could be working for themselves, earning income, and living their dreams.

For the past several years, I have been my own boss, I make my own hours, and my only need for practicing medicine again would be for medical mission's work. Imagine never having a regular 9 to 5 again, never having to duck a creditor's phone call, and being able to travel to the places you've always dreamed of.

If I was able to do this, you can also do it with your own online business. It's just a matter of knowing the right strategies, taking action to implement them, and being consistent in your efforts. That's what you're going to learn in this book.

Who This Book Is For

I'm glad you're here, and I know that soon you will be too. The fact that you're even reading this says something about you. It means that there is a winner inside of you, and all you need to know is how to play the game.

The information within the following pages has the power to change your life. I know that may sound cliché or over the top, but the concepts and resources I've included are enough to make a determined individual successful.

This book can help take you where you want to go IF you apply what it teaches consistently. IF you put in the work outlined here, you can have your own business up and running in no time.

I'm not promising retirement to Fiji, Mai Tais on a hammock, or anything like that. I'm stating a simple fact - if you put in the work to build a business, a business will be built. With the system you'll learn in this book, you can build a business that generates income 24 hours a day.

If you're looking for someone to sell you a pipe dream, then I'm afraid you will be disappointed because I don't have any to sell. What I do have is a solid, proven system that, when put into action, provides a predictable result that gets better the more you put it into practice. If that seems fair, then allow me to introduce myself.

My name is Ark Pizarro, and I am the Founder of Pizarro Consulting. I'm a digital marketer with over 12 years of experience. I specialize in paid traffic, content marketing, and email marketing. But this was not always the case, and in a little while, I will explain that further. First, let's address the elephant in the room. How exactly can a business generate income 24 hours a day?

Advancing Possibilities teaches you how to start with very little and become a full-fledged entrepreneur with a website, customers, and an income within a short period of time. All you need is a computer, an internet connection, and the determination to put in the work and win the entrepreneurship game.

Thanks to the technology we have today, your computer or phone and a few dollars are enough to get started. I'll show you how to do things for free when possible, but in reality, your time is worth more than chasing after things just because they're free.

Thousands, if not millions, of people, are doing this every day, and so can you. However, you must be willing to follow the steps I provide in this book. You must familiarize yourself with the concepts and, more importantly, put them into practice. That means you'll have to read this more than once and practice what you've learned until you get it right. If that sounds like something you're willing to do, then the sky's the limit, and you too will soon know how to build a 24 hour day online sales machine.

DISCLAIMER: I cannot guarantee you will see any results referenced in this guide in your own attempts. Your actions or lack thereof are out of my control and, therefore, your personal responsibility. I have provided clear instructions for building a successful online business. However, it is up to you to follow through with the steps and build your business. You may or may not make any money with this system. Whether you do or not entirely depends on you. By continuing to read this book, you acknowledge that you agree with everything you just read.

Obstacles

Still here? Good. The fact that you are still reading this sets you apart from the countless individuals who talk about their dreams but never do anything significant to realize them. Let's address some of the most common obstacles that may have kept you from achieving your desired success in the past.

Obstacle #1 – Not knowing where to start

By the end of this book, you will be able to say, "I know more about starting an online business than most people ever will." and "I know exactly what I need to do." I will provide you with a step-by-step formula that will help you get your business off the ground.

Obstacle #2 – Fear of failure

Fear of failure can be a huge roadblock. Fear is a powerful and often irrational emotion that can serve as a tool or a handicap. The best way to deal with it is to face it head-on. When you do, it loses its grip over you, and the experience of facing your fear empowers you.

Whenever I face my fears, the outcome is secondary compared to how good I feel about myself and how much stronger I become. It feels like leveling up in a video game.

What do you think would be the worst-case scenario if you started an online business that failed? You would probably lose a few dollars, but you'll have learned some valuable lessons in the interim. Your "failure" would provide valuable experience to avoid repeating the same mistakes in the future.

Through failure, we gain experience. That, in turn, is a benefit that is hard to put a price on. Abraham Lincoln failed to get elected to 16 public office positions before he was finally elected President. Don't be afraid to fail (in my opinion, you only fail when you quit, but that's a topic for another book).

Obstacle #3 - Economic hardship

Not having a good income isn't strange in these uncertain times, nor is it cause for shame. Above all else, it is a great motivator for rising above your circumstances and determining to work your way out of a situation no one enjoys. Instead of binge-watching shows on Netflix or sitting around complaining about this or that, get up and go to work for yourself.

If you don't have money, you can still make time and build your business with all the free resources available to us online. Is it possible? Absolutely! Can you do it? That depends on you and how dedicated you are to learning, taking action, and seeing it through.

For this to work, you have to be hungry. You have to look at yourself in the mirror and say, "You can do this! Now stop wasting time making excuses and get your butt to work and build this business!" Step by step, like bricks, form a building, your consistent effort will build your business, and from that, your dreams will start to become a reality.

Obstacle #4 – Thinking you have to be special

The media is filled with stories of tragedy, hardship, failure, etc., that program us into believing that only the gifted, the famous, the beautiful, and the wealthy can make it in this world.

We buy into this myth because we see it on TV, online, and in magazines at your neighborhood supermarket checkout line. It becomes our reality since "what you think is what you become." Well, I've got news for you! That's the first of many myths that you have been sold, and that ends right now!

What if I told you that a high school dropout from a blue-collar family, raised in the inner city of New York, went on to become a physician, teacher, and businessman. Would you believe me? Well, I am that guy... and I did. I beat the odds with lots of hard work, plenty of sacrifices, and the Almighty's grace.

I have taught executives who never missed a day of school and graduated with honors from the most prestigious universities how to run their businesses. The best part is that I get paid for doing it. So, you don't have to be an expert with a degree from Harvard, a trust fund baby with daddy's connections, or a guy with ten million followers on YouTube to "make it." Those things are great for those who have them, but you're not disqualified if you don't. Experts aren't born; they're made.

Obstacle #5 – I don't know code, design, or marketing

All of the above play a role in doing business online, but none have anything to do with you other than marketing. I'm here to teach you the steps necessary to build a profitable business through marketing.

There are software tools and people who are more than happy to do your web development and any other tasks you choose to outsource. All you need to know is what needs to get done and then pay someone to do it.

Andrew Carnegie, considered by many to be the second richest man in history after John D. Rockefeller, wanted this put on his tombstone, "Here lies a man who knew how to enlist in his service better men than himself." In essence, you don't need to know it all; just hire those who do. But you're probably thinking, "Hire? With what money?" Don't worry, we'll get into that later, and you will be amazed.

Just in case you're thinking, "this isn't for me; I'm not a marketer." I have news for you; we are all marketers! We're social marketers, to be exact. Whenever you've told a friend, they should buy the same toy you had so you could play together. That was social marketing. When your wife tells her mom, sister, or neighbor about a new store she shops at, that's social marketing. When you got her to marry you or convinced your boss, you deserved that raise... That's all social marketing!

In other words, marketing is communicating and convincing another person that your idea is best. This is no different from what you've already been doing your whole life with your friends, family, classmates, and coworkers.

Obstacle #6 – Teaching is for experts

This is definitely the obstacle that held me back the most during my own journey. I felt that I had to learn so much more before I could be a "credible" teacher/information marketer. Even though whenever I opened my mouth around business owners, they'd ask for my number and say they wanted to talk. Why? Because I hadn't realized that I was already in the top 2% of marketers in the world.

We tend to underestimate our abilities and value in the marketplace. Deep down, we're just afraid. There is no greater fear than the fear of the unknown.

That same fear breeds a need for perfection. So we tell ourselves, "it's not good enough," or "I'm still not ready." Dan Kennedy, a marketing master known for creating hundreds of millionaires through his coaching, says, "Good is good enough." So you have to start now and stop waiting to be "ready."

Let me ask you a question, "Did you read the entire manual and score 100 on your driver's exam before you actually drove your car for the first time?" I think not. Remember the first time you had to merge onto a busy highway? Most of us are pretty scared of doing that for the first time, but we did it anyway, and now we do it all the time without ever giving it a second thought. That's my point. Practice does make perfect, and over-analysis causes paralysis.

Have you ever wondered why it is that when you're in a line at the bank or the supermarket, and you voice an opinion out loud, almost everyone will look at you and agree? You know why? Because you're expressing your opinion, and since you did so while everyone else was just thinking it, you established authority and set yourself apart.

More than anything else, people want to fit in. They want to be a part of something bigger than themselves and feel important. In other words, people want to be led. So, when a leader stands out, people follow.

This phenomenon is no different when expressed through articles, podcasts, or videos. People will listen and assume you're an expert, even if you're not, because they don't know that. In time, through consistency, you will become the expert they already believe you are. Cool right?!

Obstacle #7 - It's too expensive to start a business.

When I was writing this, the buzz in the media was about the S&P 500 failing to make new highs (after hitting all-time highs a few months ago). The reality is that no matter how high the Dow Jones or S&P 500 go, people are still afraid.

They're afraid because in the back of our minds is the thought, "what if another crash happens?" Millions of average Americans are fed up with economic inequality, global instability, and the widespread fearmongering in the media.

Why do these things happen? Usually, because a handful of greedy individuals do their best to profit while hurting the system, we all trust them to safeguard. In a nutshell, people across the country are strapped for cash and unsure of what's around the corner. So, who has the extra money needed to start a business, right?

Wrong! Some of the biggest household names got their start when it seemed unwise to start a new business. Companies like General Electric (GE) got its start in what was known as the panic of 1873, a time of recession that lasted for six years.

One of the world's largest computer manufacturers, HP was started in a garage during the Great Depression. Dell, Microsoft, and Facebook were all started in college dorms. Come on! College dorms!! We all know how broke college kids are! Most of them survive on Ramen Noodles and Pizza until they graduate.

The point I'm making here is that a little cash and lots of sweat equity can get you where you want to go, regardless of how you start. With all the free tools available today, you can start a business at almost no cost. The more widespread the technology becomes, the cheaper it will get. Today, for less than $100, you can cover most of your business expenses for the first year. No, that's not a typo. I said year.

Here's a breakdown of the tools and expenses I recommend:

- Autoresponder $0 (Mailchimp gives you 2000 email subscribers - free)
- Camera and Microphone $0 (Built into to your smartphone and laptop)
- Chrome $0 (Best browser for marketing)

- Domain Name: $10 (I recommend Namecheap)
- Google Account $0 (Email/Documents/Cloud Storage)
- Hosting $5 per month (I recommend Bluehost)
- Loom $0 (Screen recording tool)
- Notetaking app $0 (Apple Notes, Google Keep, etc.)
- WordPress $0 (Free with your hosting account)
- WordPress theme $0 (WordPress offers hundreds of free themes)
- Zoom $0 (Remote meetings)

Basically, for $5 a month, you can run your online business using nothing but free tools and a paid hosting account for your website. You literally cannot use money as your excuse.

Obstacle #8 - I've failed in the past, and I'll fail again

It's sad to see how many people suffer from this way of thinking. But I have the cure for this ailment. Here it is - "your past does not determine your future." I'll say it again. "Your past does not determine your future." If you screwed up yesterday, it doesn't mean you have to screw up today. If you tried your hand at a business that failed, I'm sure you could school me on what not to do if I were going to start the same type of business.

With every so-called failure, you gain valuable experience you may have never gained otherwise. I've learned some valuable lessons over the years, and the best ones always came from my mistakes. I still have a lot to learn and a bunch of new mistakes to make. I won't be happy when I make them, but they will benefit me more than hurt me in the long term. As Seth Godin often teaches, "Fail and fail fast; failure is valuable."

I've been where you are today. I clearly remember when my marketing didn't make a red cent. I was overwhelmed, stressed out, and under a lot of pressure.

I doubted myself and grew tired of my friends and family telling me I was wasting my time and talent. But I listened to guys like Frank Kern and Jeff Johnson, who said they had gone through similar situations, and what I needed to do was work smarter and persevere. In other words, there is no resistance that can withstand persistence.

That statement inspired me. I believed what they were saying, and I did it. Now I want that for you. But you have to want it too. Remember, it's not a question of "if"; it's a question of "when." Stop saying, "If I..." and start saying, "When I..." This may seem insignificant, but it is HUGE!!

...

For as he thinketh in his heart, so is he...

PROVERBS 23:7

Mindset

Now that you know my story and we've dispelled the obstacles that you thought were in your way, it's time to get on the road that leads to your success. To do that, one of the first things we need to do is get our way of thinking in order. It's been said, "Whether you think you can, or you think you can't — you're right." To accomplish anything in life, you have to believe in your own ability to take action.

The challenges and setbacks we face sometimes leave us frustrated and confused. We ask ourselves, "What was I thinking?" Instead, we should be telling ourselves, "I'm still here, alive and kicking!" I've always liked the saying, 'What doesn't kill you makes you stronger.' It's not because it's always true, but because of the mindset it represents - defiance in the face of adversity.

Throughout history, whenever someone set out to achieve something great, they were told it wasn't possible. They called them crazy; many were persecuted and even killed. But we never remember the names of the naysayers. History remembers those who dared to dream and be different.

You currently have a unique opportunity in your possession. This guide teaches you how to build prosperity by following a plan that others have used to achieve incredible wealth. I guess that more than a roadmap; this is really a treasure map. Millions of people across the world would love to acquire this map, but most will go through life without ever knowing it even exists.

You, on the other hand, have a copy. In contrast, millions of others don't have access to clean water, indoor plumbing, or electricity, much less internet access. You, my friend, are privileged, regardless of what society tells us being privileged means. So, commit to giving this your best effort, and I guarantee that you will be surprised by the results. Facing your fears and testing your doubts are two of the greatest things we can do because they force us to grow, and that's always a win.

Here are a few quick mindset tips to get you going.

- Start small; see what works and build on that.
- 20% of your work will produce 80% of your profits. (Pareto's Principle)
- Your success is directly related to how much action you take.

Numbers, Days, and Happiness

I can't emphasize enough the importance of setting goals. They give us a clear path to where we want to be. When you find yourself in a daze, drifting along, or overwhelmed with the number of things you want to accomplish, write down your goals. Your goals will always ground you and help you refocus on what you are doing.

The following exercises will give you a clear understanding of how to get where you want to be. They will save you a great deal of time and frustration. I hope that they will help you build a better life.

Exercise #1

Write a list of the things you would do or buy if you had a multi-million dollar income. I call this knowing your number. Be specific and go 10x higher than what you believe possible.

For example:

- 2021 GMC Denali - $78,170.00 @ 72 months = $1,085 a month
- 2021 Tesla Model S - $87,990 @ 72 months = $1,223 a month
- Home in Argyle, TX - $1,225,000.00 @ 30 yrs. fixed = $5,576 a month
- 4 Trips for a family of six - $100,000.00 @ 12 months = $8,333 a month
- Private School for 4 kids - $200,000.00 @ 48 months = $4,166 a month
- Fixed expenses (food, phone, utilities, charity, etc.) - $50,000.00 @ 12 months = $4,166 a month

That's a grand total of $24,549 a month or $294,588 a year. That may seem like a lot for the average Joe, but I know people online who make 40 times that amount per month. That $24,549 breaks down to $818 a day, which is 8.4 sales of any product you offer at $97. It's really not that far-fetched once you break it down.

Now, we know that our number is $818 a day. This is what we'll be working towards with our business. This is totally doable (with practice, of course). You may be saying to yourself, "This guy is crazy!" "What is he thinking?" Some of you may not make $24,549 a year, and that's ok because I'm going to show you how to change that.

However, if you think I'm crazy, then I guess somebody didn't get the memo that money is hard to make. Did you know 2016 ended with the highest number of millionaires ever recorded in America? 10.8 million of them, to be exact! Each of these individuals had $1 Million or more (not including their main home), and 156,000 had $25 Million or more. The number of millionaires in America is projected to increase to 18 Million by 2021.1

You mean to tell me that given the proper tools and instructions, you can't do what more than 10 million people have already done? There's a formula to it, and if you follow the formula, just like a recipe, you should get the same results. Kobe Bryant became one of the greatest basketball players of all time by modeling his game after Michael Jordan's. He understood that copying what works and being ferociously consistent leads to success.

Exercise #2

Determine what you will be doing in the next 30 days, 60 days, and 90 days. Most people never plan what they'll be doing in 3 weeks, much less 90 days, which is why most people accomplish so little outside of their jobs! Write it down and tape it to your monitor, your bathroom mirror, and your fridge door, and every day give them a quick read. This will keep you focused on your goals.

Give each task a little checkmark each day when you complete them. This is super powerful for staying motivated and keeping track of your accomplishments. Focus on doing three money-generating activities each day. No busy work!

Exercise #3

This may be the most important of all because it's about living a quality life right now. Take a piece of paper, fold it in half, and title one side "Things that make me happy" title the other "Things I do daily." Now list the things that make you happy and on the other side the things you daily.

Lastly, look at the happy side and some of these items to your weekly schedule. Why aren't you doing them? Probably because you're not making them a priority. Now look at the daily side and eliminate some things that don't make money or bring you closer to your goals. It sounds simple, but when you actually do it, it's powerful.

These two easy and important steps will help ensure that you remain focused on your goals and work towards them faster and more efficiently. It's simple, and that's why it's so powerful. It's easy to do, yet so few people do it. In school, they never taught us how to plan out our lives or manage our money. Yet, we're surprised that so many people have trouble doing both.

Most people shuffle along for years going from one thing to another. They don't have a plan to follow, and sadly life happens to them. Some get lucky, but most don't. Don't feel too bad if you've been there because you don't have to be from now on.

Time Management

The early bird catches the worm. As a child, that phrase was said to me every time I complained about having to get out of my warm bed during the winter months. At the time, I didn't understand that there is no commodity more valuable than time. We have to make the most of it.

How we manage our time is a key factor in how successful we become. Have you ever seen a thriving business where the owner opens up shop whenever he feels up to it? No, and you never will. If you follow the three simple steps below, your productivity will increase significantly.

Put a value on your time.

Let's assume you know your number by now, and it's $1 Million a year. That $1 Million is equal to $2,739 per day, or $114 per hour. When someone stops you to chit chat during your workday, every minute you're not working is costing you $1.90. Is it worth it? Believe me, it isn't. Just tell them you'll catch up later and get back to work!

Follow your production calendar.

If you set aside Tuesday's for writing your book and your friends invite you out, take a rain check and stick to your plan. This is your business, and your success is a direct result of how much you produce. Do you want to get paid every month or every couple of months? You decide. I recommend setting aside blocks of time for fun. Sticking to a schedule will get more accomplished, and then your free time will be more enjoyable and guilt-free.

Remember that you want to create great products, not perfect products. When it's good, it's good enough. Don't worry about making a perfect product, website, video, etc. That kills valuable time, creates doubt and unnecessary frustration. The pursuit of perfection sounds cool in those Lexus commercials, but it's just an excuse for the average person. Pursuing perfection allows you to cover up the real reason you need it to be perfect. You're afraid, simple as that. You're scared to launch something that people will hate, ridicule, or worse, ignore.

Perfectionists are afraid to fail, and so they never win either. Remember that you can make revisions of your work down the line and sell it again as a "new and improved" version. Look at Apple; they've built a multi-billion-dollar business doing the very same thing! They launch products and improve them with updates. As a result, they are one of the most valuable companies on earth.

Share your 90-day schedule with people you respect. Let them know that your time will be limited because you are building something meaningful. Ask them to hold you accountable by reminding you of your commitment if they see you slacking off. Most of all, stick to your schedule and celebrate the small wins with something you enjoy doing on the weekend. During the week, grind it out, and on the weekend, take some time to enjoy life. Reflect on your accomplishments and the things that need improvement from the past week.

Thinking about your week is a very powerful self-observation exercise. If you can see clearly and be truthful with yourself, you will know where you are wasting time. Eliminate those activities and replace them with income-generating activities instead. There's always a way to improve if you're honest with yourself and have the discipline to follow through.

Success Modeling

Tony Robbins says, "success leaves clues." By looking at consistently successful people, you can figure out what they are doing that makes them a success. I'm laying out a system for you to follow, and that is an easier form of success modeling.

Let's imagine your neighbor Sally is really good at baking cakes, and she shares her best recipe with you. You follow her directions by getting all the ingredients you'll need. You prepare the batter, pour it into the baking pan, and place it in the oven for the amount of time she specifies. When it's done baking, it should taste as good as Sally's or very close to it.

You have successfully modeled her ability to bake a great cake. That's success modeling in a nutshell. So, why should modeling someone who makes a lot of money be any different? It's not, but we're convinced that it is!

In the case of creating a successful business, we need an insider's view of what successful entrepreneurs do. We need to see the steps they've taken, their insights, and, most importantly, their recipes. What is it that they regularly do? What steps are they taking that makes them money? Figure this out, and you will have one of the best forms of entrepreneurship training available. I'll explain this in more detail later in the book.

There is a famous saying that I often quote, "Tell me who your friends are, and I'll tell you who you are." Our lives are a reflection of the people that surround us. If you spend time with doctors and lawyers, you'll likely become a doctor or a lawyer. If you spend time with criminals, it's more than likely that "doing time" is somewhere in your future.

In short, if you want to be wealthy, spend time with people who know how to build wealth. I don't mean to go out for drinks with them. That might be too hard for some people to accomplish right now. Keep it simple; start studying the masters of wealth building and do what they do. How did they build their wealth? What was their strategy? Find it and repeat it. You will more than likely get a similar result.

Luck happens to those who take consistent action. Study the masters in any industry, and you'll see that the common trait they possess is, relying on what they know and correcting the course as they go. Unlike the rest of us, they don't waste time learning all there is to know on the topic and then get started.

Do you see how much your success is tied to the way you think, and a few good habits people are rarely taught? It's crazy! I want to share with you a critical success hack. This one is about how you talk to yourself. Self-talk can either be your superpower or your kryptonite, depending on whether it's positive or negative. We smile at everyone and say things are great when we are internally destroying ourselves with negative thoughts. I experienced this, and it held me back significantly for a long time.

When you speak to yourself and when you're trying to make decisions, ALWAYS talk to yourself in the same way you talk to a close friend in need. Assuming you are a good person, you will try to give them your best advice. Your decisions for their life will have very little emotional blurriness.

Instead, your decisions will be more precise and easier to execute. We always see everyone else's problems as easy to solve because there is very little emotional attachment. So, what we're able to see are clear winning decisions with obvious outcomes. When you start to speak well to yourself and add in stubborn determination, you will be amazed at how much you can accomplish. Try it; you are going to be amazed!

It doesn't matter how much marketing strategy and tactics you learn if you don't have a proper mindset. You'll always have a battle going on inside your head that will slow you down if not cause you to fail altogether. It's really important to read a couple of mindset books and get your mind right!

Once you do that, I want you to choose the three business people that you admire most. Read their Wikipedia page and learn their history. If they have a biography written about them, read it. Watch some videos about them and see how they describe their journey in interviews. Take notes on what they say were their most significant breakthroughs and see which ones you can apply to your journey.

It may seem trivial, but these are things that have taken countless successful people to higher heights. Repeating the success generating behaviors of people they admired. Kobe Bryant modeled Michael Jordan. Prince modeled Jimi Hendrix. Elvis modeled Little Richard, and the list goes on.

List Building

Most digital marketing books cover a list of topics like how to do niche research, domains, hosting, and email autoresponders before touching on list building. But I find that to be putting the cart before the horse since all that other stuff is generally done to support your list building efforts, which happens to be one of the most important things you can do to build your business. To me, it makes sense to cover this skill first and then explain the rest later.

List building is the first step to ensure that your business always has customers willing to open up their wallets. It's also one of the 3 principal forms of traffic online. They are the traffic you control (email subscribers), the traffic you borrow (paid ad traffic, social media), and traffic you don't control (random website visitors, affiliate traffic, etc.)

List Building is the process of getting people to sign up for your email list. This allows you to help solve the problems they face with products or services that create a profit for you and your business. The easiest and most effective way to do this is by rewarding your visitors with something of value for free in exchange for their name and email. This enacts the law of reciprocity, where they return an act of kindness for an act of kindness they received.

The things we can offer them can vary, so let's call them "lead magnets" because they help us attract leads. Your lead magnet can be a newsletter, an eBook, a video, a webinar, an audio file, a discount code, participation in a giveaway, etc. Whatever it is must be perceived as having great value. It has to offer a solution to a problem your prospective client is having.

Your prospects will see this lead magnet offer on your landing page. This is a web page designed to present the benefits of your lead magnet offer while collecting visitor names and emails in the "optin box."

Key elements your landing page must have to be effective:

- It must have a good headline.
- It must have bullet points.
- It must have a clear call to action. (a command to take action)
- It must be written with a focus on the emotions of the reader.
- It should have a sense of urgency.
- It should have a picture of a person on the page.
- It shouldn't have unnecessary links, logos, images, etc. (they lower conversions)

Your lead magnet and landing page are the foundation of lead capture and list building. They are essential for your business's growth and work in any market, even physical products. When done correctly, you can build and maintain email lists with loyal subscribers for years.

The success of your lead magnets, landing pages, and email marketing relies heavily on how well you can provoke an emotional response from the reader. Think of the best movies you've ever seen. They probably made you laugh and cry or get excited and sad before the movie ended. That rollercoaster of emotions is a big reason why they are so memorable. Because they connected to you on an emotional level, and that is what your marketing must do. You have to talk to people as if you know their pain, frustration, or passion.

Get two guys with the same team jersey in a room, and it will be almost impossible for them not to talk about their beloved sport and their most loved and hated players. The team brings them together on an emotional level. Who they are and what they do doesn't matter because they are fellow fans who understand each other.

What I am getting at is called copywriting in the marketing world. It's persuasive writing, and its goal is to direct pre-existing interest towards a particular product or service. There are lots of scammy marketers out there. Please don't be another one. Remember that it's your job to help people solve their problems and help make the world a better place. If you think that you'll make more money by being a scammer, that may be true in certain instances, but long term, you will lose more than you make. Facts.

Once you've captured some leads (names & emails), you now have an audience of potential clients you can market and sell to. You do this by understanding their problems and applying what I like to call the "3 to 1" rule. You send your audience three valuable emails that address their problem. These emails will educate and share ways to overcome those problems as quickly and easily as possible. This builds their trust in you and establishes you as an authority to your audience. I like to call this showing them "what the problem is."

Next, you send 1 email that offers them a product that is the solution to their problem. This product/service is "how" they fix the problem. That means you can sell your products and affiliate products from sellers you trust to help them solve their problems. Remember that if you pitch 'junk' to your list, they will lose faith in you, unsubscribe, and your income will take a hit. So, protect your list like you would protect your children. Ultimately, your list will help feed your children by supporting your business.

There is a well-known cliché that says, "The money is in the list." If you have a modest list of 5000 subscribers, each time you pitch them your product (using the 3 to 1 rule, of course), you can safely assume that 1% will buy what you're selling. 1% of 5000 is 50 people. Let's suppose you sold a course on how to do something you're good at for $197. This is not an outrageous amount considering that your audience knows you provide high-value information based on your previous emails to them. Those 50 sales equal 50 x $197 or $9850 before taxes (get an accountant and thank me later).

After subtracting the cost of hosting your course on a platform like Thinkific, which charges $39 per month + 5% for transaction fees, in this case, $492, it brings your total expense to $531. $9,850 - $531 = $9,319 that goes in your pocket (assuming you only make 50 sales from that email campaign). Not too shabby for building an info product and sending out a couple of emails. Not to mention that you now have 50 qualified buyers that you can sell to again and again.

Now here is the craziest part, you don't even have to create the product if you don't want to. You can hire a researcher and a writer to handle it all at a nominal cost. Clearly, the reason an email list is so powerful is that it helps you establish a relationship with your audience. Once this audience has purchased products from you, they will likely continue buying as long as you treat them right by providing outstanding value to them.

In other words, if you charge $197 for your product, it should be worth at least $500. They will recognize this and feel they have a solution to their problem and a great deal. Don't think, "but I'll be losing $303" instead, think, "I'll be selling to them and the friends and family they'll send me through referrals." Because you're providing exceptional value at a fair price, this is what reputations and trust are built on and, as a result, repeat buyers.

I mentioned earlier that the money is in the list, but the real secret is that the money is in the list you nurture; you take care of them, and they take care of you.

The 3 to 1 rule:

1st email: Your welcome email with a link to download your opt-in offer.

2nd email: Follow up to verify they downloaded your offer and add some high-value content (tips, tricks, strategies, or cheat sheet).

3rd email: Send another high-value content email (preferably a high-quality video helping them figure out their problem).

4th email: Another high-value content email that ties into a pitch for a product or service.

Then you rinse and repeat the process. Send 3 value-packed emails, and then send one high-value email that includes a pitch for one of your products. You can do this weekly or biweekly but not further out than that because you want to stay fresh in their minds. The more offers you make, the more sales you will make (do not spam them, follow the 3 to 1 rule, or you will lose subscribers for sure).

As I said earlier, we will get into the technical side of email marketing in a bit. That part is nowhere near as important as understanding these fundamentals first.

Niche Research

Before starting any business, it's good to know what the market looks like. This reduces the likelihood of things not working in your favor. Market research, or as I prefer to call it Niche research, sounds complicated, but it's straightforward once you know what it means. It's all about getting a lay of the land, so to speak, scouting ahead to see what awaits you at the next bend should you decide to start a business in that area. It's easy for those who know how to do niche research; you just have to ask and answer a few questions.

1. Is this a market that is fueled by pain, passion, or fear?
2. Can I provide a viable solution to their problem?
3. Are there others already making money in this market?

These 3 simple questions will serve as a guide to achieving your objective. If you love fly-fishing but live in the middle of the desert, opening up a fly-fishing store in your area would probably not be the best business idea. But every day, hundreds, if not thousands of people, make the mistake of opening up a business without thinking it through. The know-how required to succeed and develop a profitable long-term company is readily available but rarely accessed. That is why approximately 90% of new businesses fail within the first five years.

Market research online and offline is a bit different but have the same DNA.

Basically, opening a profitable business isn't about creating what you believe will be the next big thing. It's about giving people what they already know they want to buy, something to solve their problems. Doing this online is even easier than it is offline in your typical brick and mortar business.

Online, the consumer searches for the item they want through the search engines. I've said before that search engines are nothing more than modern-day phonebooks. Whenever someone needs a plumber, instead of using an overstuffed and antiquated phonebook, they jump onto Google and type in something along the lines of "Plumber Akron Ohio." This search phrase is commonly called a Keyword.

What is a keyword?

A keyword is a specific word or phrase used to search for a topic or item of interest on the web.

Why are keywords important?

Keywords serve as flags or markers for websites, articles, images, videos, and all the other forms of content we find online. They help us pinpoint what it is we are looking for. In return, the search engine ensures that we find the information most relevant to our search. This also helps website owners who want to optimize content so that whatever they are selling is easily found in the search results.

When we label our content (called tagging), we help the search engines filter out what's most relevant. For instance, by tagging our site with something like "plumbing services in Akron, Ohio," we're saying our site is related to plumbing services instead of a website about a man called John Plumber, who lives in Akron, Ohio.

This tagging is part of a larger field called Search Engine Optimization, or SEO. By optimizing our site's content (articles, videos, audio, images), we increase our chances of making it to Google's first page. The higher your site is on the first page of Google for that keyword; the more likely customers will visit your website. It's as simple as that.

Here is another good example; let's suppose that we are interested in building a site about baby cribs. We begin our search using 'baby cribs' as our main keyword and see what other terms (keywords) are relevant. When we get all this information, we add these keywords to our content (articles, videos, audio, images). Then, anyone who searches for that term has a better chance of visiting that content on our site. (I have simplified this a bit for the sake of clarity).

How to Choose a Niche

Those that have tried their hand at online marketing and failed are convinced that making money through the web is only for a few lucky individuals. The truth be told, most 'marketers' don't know the basics of how to market online successfully. The most critical part of online selling is knowing who you're selling to and what it is they're looking to buy. To discover these two vital pieces of information, you must do some research. I know that word may cause some of you flashbacks of your high school term papers and libraries, but it's really not that bad.

To begin your research, first, you have to choose a potential market. For your business to be successful, your niche should reflect the things you enjoy or, at the very least, things you find interesting. Expert marketers have differing opinions on this. Some say, "a product is a product," and others say, "if you hate the product, you'll hate selling it." I tend to agree with the latter.

There are three root causes for just about any problem people may face. When you drill down to the root of a problem, you will see that it is caused by pain, irrational passion, or fear. Let's do a little exercise that will help us drill down to your root problem(s). Then we'll take it from there and position ourselves in a market where we would best fit in.

Write down 3 pains, 3 passions, and 3 fears you have.

1. Out of this list of 9 items, choose the 5 with the highest priority.
2. Place these 5 items in order of priority to you.
3. Research each item in Google Keyword Planner and see what related keywords appear and their monthly search volume. (5,000 – 60,000 is best)
4. Take those keywords and combine them with words that make a memorable and easy to pronounce the name. Next, we'll check to see if the .com domain and social sites (Facebook, Twitter, YouTube, Instagram) are available for your new brand.
5. Check their availability on namechk.com (yes, namechk.com, it's not misspelled).

This may seem tedious, but it is necessary to build a brand with a solid foundation and generate income for years to come.

Keyword Tools

There are many keyword tools available to help you get the information needed to choose your brand's best keywords. One of the best, in my opinion, also happens to be free. It's called the Google Keyword Planner. The way I see it, Google has a vested interest in providing you with the best information possible so you can buy and sell their ads.

For that to happen, you will need accurate information that will effectively direct traffic to your site. That information comes from their keyword tool, and I recommend it highly since I use it regularly.

The Google Keyword Planner (GKP) provides a powerful feature that allows the user to type in a website URL (domain name), have it analyzed, and reveal what keywords are most likely being used on that website. Access to your competitor's keywords reduces the time needed to build effective keyword lists.

For example, say you want to be ranked the #1 site for golf. You enter the current #1 golf site's URL and see what keywords they use to achieve that ranking. Then you add those keywords to your website and content. Now, you have potentially improved your ranking with work that someone else did for you (figuring out which keywords to use).

The best use of this strategy is getting the URLs for the top ten results on Google for your niche. Then analyzing each of those sites by entering their domain URL into the GKP, copying the list of their best keywords, and adding them to your own website and content.

There are other keyword tools that help us determine the amount of traffic our competitors get, where this traffic is coming from, what keywords they use, and who their audience is. By knowing that most people who buy from you are middle-aged women, for example, you would know to stop any current ads that cater to young men. This is called 'knowing your demographics.'

Essentially, by knowing your audience, you are better able to cater to their specific needs. Catering to their needs will create the appropriate response you desire from them. Have you ever seen a baby formula ad on a car website? What chance is there that anyone looking at a site about cars will click on an ad about baby formula? But if that same baby formula ad was on a website about new moms or parenting, I guarantee that it would be clicked on quite a bit.

The following tools will allow you to view and copy your competitor's marketing strategies and be more competitive in your niche.

Google Trends - helps you see what people are searching for now and over time to give you ideas for niches and content creation.

Ubersuggest - helps you see where keywords are ranked, their competition level and related keyword suggestions, and much more.

Soovle - gives you keyword suggestions from sites like YouTube, Amazon, Google, and Bing.

You'll notice that all of these sites I suggest are free. There are lots of good paid tools as well. The ones that I have used and prefer are SEMrush and Ahrefs. Both are solid tools with good track records and strong teams behind them. However, I don't recommend using paid tools unless your business is already making money and you can justify the expense. If you're just starting out, you do not need them.

Another thing to note is that Google gives you this data for free. In contrast, these tools get data from Google and a few other sources and repackage it and charge you a monthly fee. Sometimes the user experience is better; for some, the customer support and training are better, but overall, they are not a necessity.

Below is a breakdown of the strategies we just discussed.

How to research your target market:

1. Find the top ten websites for your niche by searching for your main keyword on Google. For instance, "fly fishing" The first ten results for that keyword are the only ones we're interested in (ignore the ads).
2. Take those website addresses (URL) from the top ten results and analyze them one by one in the Google Keyword Planner. Copy the keywords that are the most relevant (5000 - 60,000 monthly searches).
3. Visit their websites and see what kind of content (articles, video, audio,

images, and ads) they have. Take good notes so that you have a shortcut to what you know is already working when you create your site's content.

4. Take notes on the kinds of ads they have on their sites. This gives you an idea of who advertises in your niche and will help you find advertisers and affiliate offers for your website.

5. Check to see if they have significant followings on Facebook, YouTube, and Instagram. If so, what are they doing that's building their fan base? What type of things are they posting about? What are their videos about? What hashtags do they use most? If they don't have a strong social presence, you can easily beat them by building one for your brand.

6. Lastly, what kind of traffic is there for social media sites in your niche? Are there only a few videos or many? Are there lots of community groups or none?

All this vital information will reveal whether you're choosing a good niche or not. It will help you 'Reverse Engineer' your competitor's success. Keep in mind that the internet in 2020 is mature, so if there isn't a lot of content or competitors in your niche, it's probably not going to be a very good niche.

Reverse Engineering is studying what someone else has created by taking it apart and examining the parts. If you 'reverse engineer' someone else's steps to creating a successful website and brand, you'll know how to build one for yourself.

Clickbank Research

Our last step in researching a niche market is done in the Clickbank Marketplace. Clickbank is a website that serves as a marketplace for digital information products. It is also a shopping cart service for the sellers of these products. They offer a wide selection of products and have a good track record going back several years. Clickbank is an excellent source for niche research and selling online when you're first starting.

To determine if your niche is available on Clickbank, you will open up an account and go to the marketplace and search, for example, "golf." This will show you the products related to golf and the sales page(s) that product sellers have created. Then, as discussed earlier, take their URL and drop it into the GKP to see what keywords they're using and check out their online presence to see how they've built their brand.

If we're convinced it's a product that will sell, we can advertise this Clickbank product on our website and generate additional revenue. A very ninja way of doing this is by testing out a niche product on your site.

If it sells well, make a product of your own (outsourcing the product creation), then replace the current ads with ads for your own product and keep 100% of the profit. This has worked for some of the biggest names in internet marketing. By using this very technique, they make millions each year.

With Clickbank, you'll pay around $50 to promote your own information product(s), but they handle most of the customer service for you. If you prefer free product listings for your info products and you don't mind handling your own customer service, then checkout JVZoo.

Brand Creation

Domains

I call this chapter brand creation because it covers the building blocks needed to get your business up and running online. There are several steps that must be taken whenever you're starting a web-based business. I've gone ahead and narrowed it down to the essential steps. This will help you begin as soon as possible and avoid a lot of the busywork that people get wrapped up in (perfecting their website or surfing social media for info), and actually, start something that matters.

For people to find you online, you will need a domain name (www.example.com). It should be related to your keyword, and it should be a dot com. If the site is about baby cribs, we would like something along the lines of www.thecrib.com as our domain name. The exact keyword domains like babycrib.com used to be great for ranking in Google until Google released an update that made it bad to have an exact match domain name. Later they revised that update, but in my opinion, exact match domains should be avoided and instead focus on building an original keyword related brand name.

The chances of an exact match domain name being available for purchase are slim to none anyway since most of those types of names have been taken for years. We would probably have to consider a name such as www.babycribpros.com, or something along those lines. I always purchase my domains from Namecheap. I've used their service for about ten years, and I have always been satisfied with their reliable service and frequent discounts.

You'll notice that our keyword is "baby cribs." It's our keyword because it's the term people will search for when they're interested in purchasing a baby crib. By including a part of our keyword in the domain name, we are trying to give the people a memorable brand that they'll think of when looking to buy a baby crib.

You can choose to focus your writing on the search engines, or you can write for the people who use the search engines. I prefer to write for people because people engaging with your site will always improve your search rankings in the long run.

This is the beginning of an ongoing game to have the highest rank in the Search Engine Results Page (SERP). It is better known as the art and science of Search Engine Optimization (SEO). Search engines such as Google are the modern-day phonebooks of years gone by, but the aim to be the first or the most prominent ad that people see is still the same. There is a lot that can be said about domains and SEO, but that's beyond the scope of this book.

Hosting

Your future business requires a first-rate and reliable web hosting service. What is a web host? A web host is a company that rents out space on their servers (specialized computers used for storing websites) so you can 'host' your site online. You might be asking, "Why can't I just do this from my home computer?" You can, but there are drawbacks, and it requires lots of know-how.

For instance, back in the day, people did just that, but their entire website would disappear each time they turned off their computer. Things have come a long way since then, but it still requires a good amount of technical expertise to do your own hosting. Add to that the amount of time needed to manage your own hosting. Personally, I wouldn't recommend this to anyone unless they were doing it to run their own web host company.

There are thousands of different hosts with hundreds of different features, price points, and services. So, what should you look for in a good web host? Number one in my book is reliability. You're looking to build a small business free from the headaches of countless hours trying to get your website to work. Uptime is king.

If 'uptime is king,' then customer service is the heir to the throne. Whenever something goes wrong, you want a company that will take responsibility and quickly resolves whatever issue you're having with your server.

One of the most vital elements of your website is speed. Google has added site load speed to its ranking requirements, and if your site takes more than 2 seconds to load, it will be penalized in the search results for being slow. This makes a fast hosting service an absolute must.

Scalability is also very important; you need a host that can handle traffic spikes for all those times your content goes viral, right?! It also comes in handy when your site starts getting a bunch of new visitors. Your web host should be able to handle growth without any headaches.

Last but not least is the price; you want all of the benefits mentioned above at a fair price. This is why I prefer Bluehost as my budget web host. They offer a great hosting service that is perfect for someone just starting out. As an incentive, Bluehost will throw in a free domain name when you sign up with them. This way, you get to skip buying your first domain name from Namecheap.

I like a few more advanced and more expensive web hosts, but they're more than what you need right now. If you'd like to skip the whole hosting issue and strictly focus on the business, leaving all the technical stuff to someone else, then take a look at Clickfunnels. They do all the heavy lifting and let you focus on your content and marketing.

Autoresponders

To build a list of prospective clients, you will need an email service called an Autoresponder. This email service lets you send automated messages by email to your clients. For example, every time someone signs up to your list, they will receive your welcome email. You write it once, but potentially thousands of people will receive it through signups for your newsletter, free report, or whatever your lead magnet is.

There are tons of different autoresponder services out there. If free is your thing, start with Mailchimp, and you can upgrade later as your list grows. I recommend Aweber for its ease of use and the fact that it's one of the industry originals. I've used them for years, and their service has always been solid. They also happen to be one of the most affiliate friendly autoresponders out there. If you plan on promoting affiliate products, that is a big deal since some autoresponders will shut down your account for promoting affiliate offers, and just like that, your list and income are lost.

Website

So, you have a domain name, a web host, and you signed up for an autoresponder service, now what? Now we build your site. The first thing you have to do is sign into your web host account with the login info (username and password) you were emailed when you first signed up. If you followed my advice and signed up with Bluehost, this will be easy. If not, you'll have to adjust to your own web host settings, but it shouldn't be much different. Go to your dashboard and click "WordPress."

You will be taken to your site's admin area, where you can see it live online. Pick a free theme at the WordPress theme marketplace under the Appearance tab or get the theme I use (Shapeshift) at thrivethemes.com. Start jotting down ideas about the content you want to create and follow the rest of the steps in this guide.

Remember that the content you create should answer the questions the people in your niche have. This will eliminate the guesswork of what kind of content to create, and it's easy to find in any number of forums, Facebook groups, LinkedIn groups, Reddit, and Quora. People go to these places to ask questions about the things they care about; find the ones related to your niche and jot down the most common questions you see people asking. That is what you write about on your blog.

Business Models

So, we've covered a lot of ground. Now I want to share what I consider the three best business models to implement based on their potential profitability and the number of success stories each has had over the years. Each of these systems has been proven to work for countless people across a multitude of niches and will continue to do so for the foreseeable future.

I'll start with the easiest and end with the most advanced of the three. This is not to say that there are only 3 business models you can do online; I just find these three to have the highest chance of success for someone who has never done them before. I recommend that you learn one at a time by doing them successfully a few times and then move on to the next if you want to.

The fact that you master one of these models doesn't mean you have to move on to a new business model. Whether you decide to or not is strictly a matter of personal choice. However, don't fail at one model and then jump to the next, hoping to succeed.

If, at first, you don't succeed, try and try again, as the saying goes. Figure out why you failed and ask your peers in the numerous forums and groups online what they've done to overcome similar issues. The web is full of knowledgeable people willing to help you solve a problem; ask them.

First Business Model: Niche Sites

A niche (also called affiliate) site is a website that provides relevant information about a topic and usually has affiliate offers (ads) spread around the site. The essence of these sites is to provide information to the visitor and get them to click on an advertisement or sign up for an offer.

An affiliate is someone who brings a customer to a business and gets a commission for their effort. There are different ways commissions are structured, but the most common way is what I just described. If someone clicks an ad on your website, that will take them to the advertiser's website, and you will be credited with that lead and paid within 30-90 days.

Some sites use a mix of affiliate offers and Google AdSense ads. AdSense is basically Google's own affiliate ad network. An affiliate ad network is a business that connects advertisers and publishers. The advertiser might be a cola brand, for example, and you are the publisher (the affiliate) who promotes the cola brand on their website and gets paid whenever someone clicks on the ad.

That's a simplified description, but it's good enough for now. Google AdSense used to be all the rage years ago. Today, in most marketing circles, people will roll their eyes if you mention AdSense. However, it is still a viable way to generate income, especially when you're just starting out.

If you find that your affiliate ads get more attention from your visitors, focus on those ads, and optimize your pages to get the best results. If, instead, you find that AdSense gives you the best results, then focus on optimizing those ads.

The method I use for my sites is as follows; I put my affiliate ads high up on the page in the most prominent areas. Then I put the AdSense ads lower down the page since the visitor is more likely to leave if they're getting further down the page and haven't clicked on my affiliate ads.

Some might ask, "Aren't the AdSense ads going to show the viewer competing affiliate ads?" To which I answer "probably." But it doesn't really matter since they've already seen my preferred offers higher up on the page and ignored them. My hope is that if they're going to leave, they can do it by clicking on an AdSense ad and still get me a commission.

When you build a site, you want to put about 30 high-value articles on it; you can write them yourself or pay someone to do it for you. I prefer to do them myself if it's a niche I'm familiar with. If not, I'll usually outsource them to someone on textbrokers.com or upwork.com. You can also use fiverr.com to find writers as well.

When I write the articles, I do so using the voice recorder app on my phone. You can also use the notes app on the iPhone or Evernote, etc. The transcription accuracy these days is about 90-95%. So, the writing is done for you, and all you have to do is talk about your topic and then go back and edit the transcription later.

Never edit when you are creating. It slows down the process immensely and also hinders your creativity. Just focus on creating your article and edit the next day when you have some time away from the content you just created. You will see it from a different perspective and pick up on errors much faster.

If you're the traditional sit at a keyboard type, that works too. If you prefer to create videos and have them transcribed, there is an app I love called Descript that will take the audio from your video and transcribe it for you as well.

Needless to say, there are several ways to create content for your niche site. It's just a question of preference and budget. The reason I recommend 30 articles is two-fold. When a visitor comes to your site and sees dozens of articles, it lets them know that your website is legit (everyone is wary of scam sites). When done right, each of those articles will answer a question that people have regarding your niche.

For example, if your site is about fishing, a common question people will want answered is, "what is the best fishing pole to buy?" That's an easy article to write. You can create something like "The top 5 fishing poles for every budget." You're answering a common question, and it will draw traffic to the site for years as long as you update it every year or so. It's also a great way to add affiliate links to your article as each of the fishing poles can link back to amazon and get you a commission if they buy after they clicked through from your article. I'll discuss amazon's affiliate network a bit more later.

It is also a clear sign to the search engines that you are serious and here to stay when they crawl your website and see dozens of long-form (2000 words or more) articles that someone invested the time to create. That helps them see you as an authority site, which improves your search result rankings over time and brings you more traffic (visitors) to your site. By the way, 2000-word articles only take 20-30 minutes of speaking to create. Which is why I prefer to speak my articles and then just transcribe them with Descript.

After that, you'll want to give it a couple of months to see how the site performs. Initially, most of the traffic you get will be from whatever promotional efforts you put in to spread the word about your website. Over time if the content is of good quality, people will start to share and find you.

If the site starts to make money after two or three months, I'll add more articles, optimize the ads, and maybe add some videos to make the site more appealing. As the site continues to generate income, I'll continue to optimize it. Some websites can become a hit seemingly overnight, and others can take months before they gain any traction. It's like music artists; they never really know what song is going to be their next hit.

On the other hand, if the site doesn't build any traffic with my standard efforts,

I'll check up on it monthly and see if it changes. If not, at the end of a year, I move on. There are too many opportunities available to waste time on poor performing niche sites. You can just turn off the website, or you can try to see if anyone is willing to buy it from you on Flippa.com.

To get started with AdSense, you'll need your Gmail account to sign up for AdSense. You'll also need to sign up for Google Analytics to measure the traffic performance of your site. To join other affiliate networks is a bit harder but not impossible. You can see a list of the easier ones to join later in this chapter.

The greatest thing about this whole process is that you only have to write one niche related article per day for 30 days; that's basically 20-30 minutes a day. In my opinion, the best way to do it is to read three articles or watch three short videos on the topic and then just record yourself talking about the topic as if you were describing it to a friend.

Better yet, give a close friend a call, record it, and just tell them about what you learned, the ideas will flow, and you will easily have more than 30 minutes of content to transcribe. So, in total, the research and article creation shouldn't take you more than an hour or so per day once you get the hang of it.

There are a few basic SEO rules you should adhere to in order to help your article rank better in the search results. Your article should mention your main keyword (baby crib, fly fishing, etc.) at least 5-6 times but in a natural conversational tone. You should include 6-8 images to your articles to break the sea of text on a page.

Remember "social marketing"; you want the reader to feel like they're having a conversation with a friend. The article should be between 2000 to 3000 words long. Longer articles are better because most people won't write such a long article unless they are an authority on the subject. That line of thinking is part of how the search engines rank websites, and you can use it to your advantage.

Not only do longer articles help with SEO, but they also provide the reader with a better experience as long as they are well written. Three thousand words of garbage will do no better than 100. People just won't read it, and they won't revisit your site either, so remember, first impressions are important.

If you Google "niche site example" and click the image tab, you'll see lots of examples of what a niche site looks like. You should rearrange your ads based on what your metrics prove are the best places for each advertisement based on CTR (click-through rate).

Be aware that Google's terms of service change periodically, and with it, the number of ads that can be shown on any one page. You can currently place unlimited AdSense ads on a web page provided that the total number of AdSense ads or third-party ads does not exceed the visible content.

Maybe you're thinking, "but I can't write to save my life." You just need to transform your thinking. Go to Fiverr, Upwork, or Textbroker and pay someone $5 to $15 to write the article. Of course, you get what you pay for, so don't expect to get a $15 article with super high quality. The higher the quality of the article and the longer the article, the higher the price will be, so keep that in mind. That's also why I prefer to create my own.

Another easy way to add content to your site is by creating commentary articles on niche related news. Quote the news story, add your opinion about the topic, and link it to the article's original source or video. You can find these articles by creating keyword alerts on Google Alerts and Twilerts.

Both services are very similar in that they bring relevant keyword results to your inbox. You can just read through their results and add whatever articles you find of high value to your site. They are very powerful tools for leveraging your time and content creation. It isn't long-form content, but some content is better than none, especially after you already have your 30 long-form articles.

Some of the web's biggest sites are news aggregators, Mashable, Huffington Post, Drudge Report, etc.; they all aggregate news and the search engines don't penalize them for it. As long as you add your own valuable original content (commentary), the search engines will crawl your site and reward you for having more relevant content.

If you're going to build niche sites, these are the essential affiliate programs you should sign up for to get your feet wet.

- Amazon Associates Affiliate Program
- ClickBank Affiliate Program
- eBay Partner Network Affiliate Program
- Rakuten Marketing Affiliate Program
- ShareASale Affiliate Program

There are plenty of other affiliate programs, but they are generally much harder to get into, and that is a training course unto itself. Suffice it to say that they prefer experienced marketers who are good at PPC (pay per click advertising) and converting traffic into sales (both of which take time to master). We want to get you started right away, and with that in mind, all of the networks listed above allow you to do that, and when you get good can provide a nice income.

There are four important things to consider when choosing an affiliate network.

1. Ease of use
2. Offerings
3. Support
4. Payments

If an affiliate network or advertiser makes it difficult to get your banner images or support from your affiliate manager, that is a red flag. If they mess with my money, that's a deal-breaker. I'm a reasonable person with reasonable expectations. Giving people 24-48 hours to get back to me isn't ideal, but I can live with it. More than that, and I just feel like that is bad business. The networks I've listed above have been around for a long time. The larger they are, the more patience you'll need, but generally, they will take care of you.

When you become a more advanced marketer, you may run into networks that aren't as friendly. If that should happen, remember to always negotiate from a position of power. The guy that wins is the one who is willing to walk away first.

Let's go over a quick summary of each of these networks.

Amazon Associates Affiliate Program

- Ease of use: Great for new affiliates. Everyone knows and trusts the Amazon brand. Easy to use affiliate dashboard and link creation.
- Offerings: Millions of physical and digital products to choose from.
- Support: Amazon's support is reliable and helpful.
- Payments: Conversion rates are high. Commission rates are low. Payouts are 60 days after a sale. Payouts can be direct deposit, check, or gift certificates.

ClickBank Affiliate Program

- Ease of use: The place for affiliates who prefer promoting digital products. Very rarely need approval to promote an offer. You can promote offers without having your own website.
- Offerings: Millions of digital products to choose from.
- Support: Clickbank support is good; they are rated A+ by the Better

Business Bureau.

- Payments: Very flexible payment schedules, recurring monthly commissions are available for some products, and payouts can be direct deposit, wire transfer, or Payoneer (international affiliates).

eBay Partner Network Affiliate Program

- Ease of use: Everybody knows how to use eBay.
- Offerings: More than 1 Billion products to promote, and millions are new. They have the market cornered on unique one of a kind products.
- Support: Support is done by actual eBay employees.
- Payments: Commission rates are high. Payouts are by direct deposit or PayPal.

Rakuten Marketing Affiliate Program

- Ease of use: Best for affiliates who are ready to step up their game.
- Offerings: 1000+ household name brands to choose from. Your site will need some traffic to get approved.
- Support: Multiple awards for being the best affiliate network and rated A+ by the Better Business Bureau.
- Payments: Payments are slow like Amazon, so expect 60+ days to receive your commission. Payouts are by direct deposit, check, and PayPal.

ShareASale Affiliate Program

- Ease of use: One of the best networks out there for affiliates who want to sell a vast array of products from well-known brands without having to be signed up to multiple networks.
- Offerings: Thousands of products and services from high-quality mer-

chants to choose from (some pay as much as $300 a sale).

· Support: Solid reputation with A+ Rating from the BBB.
· Payments: 30-day payment schedule and payouts by check, wire transfer, and direct deposit.

Second Business Model: Membership Sites

This next model is a bit more advanced, but it can be highly profitable and more predictable. The major hurdle that must be overcome with this model is that it requires more preparation. On the other hand, it's a business model that can provide a very nice income for a long time because it is based on the continuity model meaning the users pay each month to continue using the service.

Membership sites are websites where you provide knowledge of a particular niche and continually add to it with new content and question and answer sessions. Users usually add a great deal of content and value to the website in comments, forum posts, and the relationships they form with other members.

The people who sign up for your member site will look to you to lead them to the knowledge they need to solve their problems. This can be done easily by choosing a niche you're highly knowledgeable in or hiring an expert to assist you in creating the site's content.

A membership site, on average, will probably take about 1 to 3 months to prepare and should have at least 12 pieces of quality content before you launch it. If you start your site with unorganized or minimal content, you're likely to increase your refund rate, and the word will spread that your website isn't worth joining.

Keep in mind that you always want people to feel that you've over-delivered.

They will quickly recognize the value they're getting and stay with you as loyal customers. I think it's best to have 1 or 2 full courses that you could charge for on sites like Clickbank in your member site, proving the immediate value your member site offers.

For example, if you're going to build a membership site around furniture carpentry, you might create a course about building chairs and a second course on table making. When you launch your member site, the new users will find those courses in the training section. They will recognize that those courses alone justify the price of the membership.

By including 1 or 2 courses and your personal responses to their questions, you will be justifying the monthly investment from the moment they signup. Be sure to include different content formats, including audio, video, and pdf, since we all consume content differently; making this easy goes a long way towards customer satisfaction.

If you think this is just too much work, here's an easy way to get some really good content. Decide upon your niche and get the 30 best videos you can find on YouTube regarding the most commonly asked questions within that niche. Then you arrange those videos within your member site in a logical order and provide transcripts of the videos (you can outsource all of this). Then answer whatever questions may arise as your subscribers ask them on your site's forum.

This is entirely legal and a valuable resource well worth $30 to $50 a month. If you're wondering how we can charge if it's available for free on YouTube, the answer is it's because they are there to solve a problem. You've provided 30 ways to solve their problem without them having to spend countless hours sifting through junk to find the gems that you provide for them.

You are providing a service, and they gain access to your efforts by joining your membership. Keep in mind you can't do this with private content like someone else's blog or membership. The content has to be from a free source like YouTube that allows you to repost their content.

Most of us could change our own oil if we needed to, but that hasn't stopped us from going to Jiffy Lube. How many people can make a burger better than McDonald's? I'd say most people, yet they're a billion-dollar company because they sell more than burgers; they sell convenience. You get the point, convenience costs...

After your member has used the site for a while, they'll form relationships with you and other users and stay on to keep in contact with their new friends. Most membership site users will usually stay subscribed for 4 to 6 months, but some sites keep their users for as long as 2 to 3 years.

One of the best ways to hold on to your users is by providing them fresh content. Question and answer webinars are a great way for them to interact with you and ask you questions in a live setting. Be sure to include webinars on your member sites. They are vitally important, and people love them.

So how do you build your member site? Of course, my first suggestion is to use WordPress with a membership plugin like Member Mouse or MemberPress. These plugins create a gateway between your content and the general public. Only paying customers can access the areas of the site you specify. Both have been around for several years and are used by many successful membership sites.

My next suggestion is your forum platform. This is where your users will communicate with each other, and IPBoard is a good choice. Some of you might think, "why not just use a Facebook group for that?" My answer is because Facebook owns and thereby controls it. Would you give a stranger the keys to your business? Because when you make your customers communicate on a Facebook group, that gives Facebook the power to just come along and say you violated a policy and shut it down.

Then what? Now your users have nowhere to engage, all of their posts are lost forever, and you're scrambling to keep up with the complaints and find a new solution. That will lead to cancellations and affect your bottom line. So, don't put your horse in the race; own the racecourse.

Meaning, avoid all that and buy software and run it yourself or with your team if you get to that size. If you're concerned about price, you have to understand that there is a cost to doing business that's simply unavoidable. As you may have already realized, I always try to show you the most economical way to get things done.

However, with all of these solutions, if you've created a value-packed site and you charge $30 or more per month, the software will pay for itself by the time you reach ten customers. Earlier I mentioned a done for you solution that allows you to build your sites with minimal technical difficulty: Clickfunnels.

However, when it comes to member sites, my preference is Thinkific. I recommend Thinkific because, like Clickfunnels, they handle all the technology and allow you to focus on your content creation. Thinkific also offers a free version for up to 10 customers. That is pretty amazing since it provides you the freedom to get comfortable with the platform before spending a dime.

Each one of these solutions is good enough to help make your member site a success. Ultimately which solution is best will depend on price and personal preference. I suggest you give them a test drive and decide which you find best for your business.

Third Business Model: Ecommerce

The final business model we'll be covering is also the most advanced, in my opinion. It's familiar to us all as we have been on the customer side repeatedly. The model I'm referring to is an e-commerce store. This is where you have a product(s) to sell, and you conduct your transactions through a website.

There are tons of platforms you can use to accomplish this task, and I'll mention my personal preference in a moment. Maybe you'd like to know why I consider this option the most advanced. Unlike all the ecom marketers out there saying you can get a successful store up and running in 24 hours and make millions, I prefer to be real with you.

Although some of those things are possible (for experienced marketers), there are several reasons why ecom is more advanced. Primarily the learning curve for mastering ecommerce is higher than the other models I've mentioned. The number of moving parts it takes to run an online store is by far greater. Am I saying it's impossible?

Absolutely not, only that if you want to go the fast and easy route (if there is such a thing), this is not it. Like all the business models we've discussed, you will do all the steps I mentioned in Brand Creation (Chapter 5) unless you use an ecommerce platform like Shopify. Personally, I prefer Shopify; they have become the leader in ecommerce because their sites are easy to use with tons of different store designs and apps to choose from.

In many ways, they copied WordPress's playbook on how to build a successful software brand. Speaking of WordPress, WooCommerce is an ecommerce platform built on WordPress, and it's one of Shopify's main competitors. Unlike Shopify, you can start a WooCommerce shop for free. As always, you'll pay the difference in price with your time as WooCommerce is a bit more hands-on.

I have been fortunate enough to make over six figures using Shopify sites, and they work well. If you're up to the challenge, ecommerce can be extremely lucrative, but as I stated, it has a high learning curve to get it right. You'll need to handle marketing, product selection, suppliers, fulfillment, shipping, and customer service, to name a few. Depending on the product, this can range from easy to difficult. On the other hand, if you're going to be selling a product that you create yourself, that can make life a lot easier. So long as you can meet the production demand once you're able to get sufficient traffic to your site.

The easiest way to manage an online store is to sell digital products like eBooks, videos, audio, and images. There's no shipping involved, you can sell multiple copies per day, and the store is open 24 hours a day, making sales all on its own. Avoid selling electronics as they have high return rates and can also have nightmarish customs issues.

If you can't go the digital products only route, try to focus on selling things with no moving parts. Things made from a block of wood, a block of metal, a block of rubber, etc. They have very low failure rates, which means more happy customers and fewer headaches for you.

For any of these business models to work in this day and age, you need to build a name for yourself and attract attention to your brand. There are some essential skills you should master if you want to build a following around your brand. We've already covered list building. Because once you have a list of potential clients, your chances of success greatly increase. Which brings us to...

...

Real artists ship.

STEVE JOBS

Content Creation

I salute you for having read up to this point. You are officially one of the few people who actually read a book from cover to cover. Reaching this point is a good indicator of the chances for your success, as it shows your determination to get what you want. I admit that I was just like you when I first started out. I devoured everything I could get my hands on and would read and re-read the same material to make sure I'd captured what the authors were teaching me.

What we'll cover next is easily worth $1000 all by itself. It's a system that helps you create products that can bring in millions over the course of your lifetime. So, consider this my gift to you for being committed. This section will not only help you create your opt-in offer; it will also help you create the products you'll be selling to your prospects for the foreseeable future.

How People Become Experts

It's very straightforward; they say that they're experts. Period. How often have you applied for a job and had someone say, "I need to see your degree." Never? Exactly. A few years ago, my wife was invited to attend a medical conference. They sponsored her to stay at the hotel, and I tagged along.

When we arrived, I paid for my reservation, picked up the keycard to the suite, and was ready for some rest and relaxation. Then, my wife asked me to join her for the first lecture. I reluctantly agreed.

When we reached the door to the conference, a medical rep stopped us, gave my wife a bag full of swag, and asked her to sign in. The rep then asked if I was also a physician or a guest. My wife said, "He's my guest, and he's also a physician." The lady said, "ok," and let us in.

During the break, the rep approached us and said that her company would sponsor my stay at the hotel since I was also a physician. She proceeded to give me back the money I paid at the front desk. I thanked her and spent a great weekend at a 5-star hotel without spending a dime!

All because I "said" that I'm an expert. No tests, no questions, no asking to see my credentials. People will generally believe you until you give them a reason not to. Mind you, I didn't have to lie, and you shouldn't either. This business is about getting people to trust you, so be worthy of that trust.

I know you might be saying to yourself, "I'm not an expert at anything," "this can't possibly apply to me." Well, I have a fix for that. Here are a few eye-opening facts about the average American.

- 57% of new books are not read to completion.
- 58% of the US adult population never reads another book after high school.
- 42% of college graduates never read another book after college.
- 70% of U.S. adults haven't been inside a bookstore in the last 5 years.
- 78% of the titles published come from the small/self-publishers.

After seeing these statistics, does it really seem that hard to be classified as an expert? Finally, perception is reality. That's why people wear suits to interviews, they want to be perceived as professionals, and the suit gives them an image that says, "I am of high value." It's not necessarily true, but that is the message wearing a suit to an interview is supposed to convey. The next time you think you're not an expert, just remember how easy it is to be an expert at something.

Note: You don't need anyone's permission to share your expertise. If you still believe that you do, I now grant you permission to share your knowledge with the world. So, get busy!

How to Make an Expert Product

Let's assume that you're not an expert (even though we are all experts at something). Here's an easy formula for becoming one. First, by following the same steps we discussed in niche research (Chapter 4), determine what you want to be an expert in. Then go to Amazon and look up books in the category for your niche. Find the best-selling books with the best reviews (at least 10 reviews) and buy the 3 bestsellers. By the way, you can save some money buying the kindle version or see if they're available at your local library instead.

As you read, each book take notes of the most important points in each chapter. The notes should be in list form with the pros and cons. For example, are you provided with sufficient images to give you a good idea of what is being explained? Is the author's writing style easy to understand? Is the information accurate? (You'll know by reading and comparing with the other books.) Is the information presented in a way that helps to learn the concepts? What kind of artwork do they use, if any?

Asking these questions will help you craft an excellent product. You'll repeat these steps for each of the three books, and from your three lists, you'll build upon the pros you read and improve upon the cons. This will make you the author of a product that is superior to Amazon's best sellers.

Even though you may not have been an expert, you used the work of other "experts" to inspire an expert product of your own, and that effectively makes you an expert too.

Please note I am in no way saying you should plagiarize anything! I am saying to note and use the works you'll study as inspiration to create an entirely original product of your own. I hope that's clear. If you should decide to copy another author's work, then be prepared to spend some time in court.

Another point that warrants addressing is publishing. I am not saying you should write a book and then try to find a publisher because, in my opinion, that would be a mistake. You'll work your butt off and get scraps from the publisher, even with a bestseller. I'm saying you should create your book and sell it online. Pocketing 100% of $10 as opposed to 10-15% of $15 is, without a doubt, a lot smarter.

So, here's a quick and easy way to write your book.

- Write an outline with 10 chapters.
- Give each chapter a title for the topic it will cover.
- Each chapter will contain 10 points that will be explained.
- Each point will consist of 1-2 paragraphs.

After you've written these 10 points for each of the 10 chapters, you'll have a resource of 100 points that will enlighten your readers and make your work credible. You are now a bonafide author, and as we all know, authors are experts, right?

So, instead of being Jane Doe, you'll be introduced as Author and Expert, Jane Doe, able to demand higher compensation for your time and energy, speak at conferences, and state your opinion on local radio and TV programs, etc. This may all seem pretty far-fetched to you right now, but it is doable.

If you don't believe this works, read the 3 bestsellers we mentioned, make your pros and cons list, and then talk to some family members, friends, and co-workers about that subject. I bet you none of them will know half as much as you do about that topic, and they'll be amazed and ask you, "When did you learn all that?" Try it!

Note: Don't go reading three Tom Clancy novels and think you're a master spy! The books must be niche related, for instance, books about photography, parenting, vegan diets, dog training, etc.

This same method applies to creating courses, member sites, podcasts, and YouTube channels as well. Content is content regardless of the format you express it in. You are simply transmitting ideas from your mind to someone else's.

Video Content Creation

This section is about one of my favorite topics, video. The reason I like video so much is that it's such a powerful communication tool (regardless of your level of expertise).

Give these facts some thought:

- People are twice as likely to share video content with their friends than any other type of content.
- 84% of people say that they've been convinced to buy a product or service by watching a brand's video.
- 87% of video marketers say video has increased traffic to their website.
- 80% of video marketers say video has directly helped increase sales.
- 89% of video marketers say video, in general, gives them a good return on their investment.

I learned the power of video when I uploaded some tutorials about WordPress in Spanish! I was just learning how to do a screencast and had no idea how much it would grow and the impact it would have at the time.

The first video I uploaded onto YouTube was over 10 years ago, and in just a few months, it had over 70,000 views. Keep in mind, this video was in Spanish, and it was about WordPress. In short, as I'm sure you already know, video is an excellent tool for promoting yourself, building a following, and your brand.

Here are some of the main reasons why.

- It builds your credibility.
- It can be promoted by others and potentially go viral.
- It establishes you as an authority and creates fans of your content.

I know that you already know this, but are you using it to your advantage? How many people actually do? Few. YouTube is full of people doing stuff. But, considering the world's population, in reality, it's only just a few people. When you stop to think about how many are doing it well, that number is dramatically smaller.

To set yourself apart from the rest of the folks online, you need to nail down some key elements. For instance, what constitutes a great video? It should contain something humorous, daring, and/or unexpected or provide value with answers and solutions.

For your videos to be effective, follow these tips:

1. Have an attention-grabbing title. Not clickbait, but intriguing.
2. Write down your main ideas, plan out what you will say, and look straight into the camera as if talking to your friends. It takes some practice for it

not to feel weird, but it is so worth the effort.

3. Keep your video length around 5 minutes. The key is to solve the viewer's problem. If that takes 10 minutes, fine. Just don't take 10 minutes to say what could have been said in 5 minutes.

4. Tag your video with keywords related to what you discuss in the video. You can use tools like Tubebuddy or VidIQ to see competitor tags and stats.

5. Always answer as many comments on your video as you can. This develops relationships with your viewers.

6. Livestreams are your friend. The algorithm loves them, and viewers do too. Super chats are a nice way to gain some extra cash.

To distribute and promote your videos, be sure to repurpose and share them on Facebook, LinkedIn, Instagram, Pinterest, and Reddit (in relevant subreddits). Post them on your blog, in relevant forums, and in whatever niche related sites you know of. We're just scratching the surface here, but it's enough to get you started, and that's the point.

Traffic Generation

Let's talk about reaching out to people online and doing some lead generation. If you don't know what lead generation is, it means drumming up business, attracting people who could be interested in what you have to offer. Whether it's visiting your website and signing up for your lead magnet or browsing the products you offer and hopefully making a purchase.

Whatever you're trying to promote, you need people to see it (traffic generation). Then you need to turn those people into customers (conversions). In essence, that is lead generation, and you need traffic (website visitors) to do that effectively.

Your job is to get in front of people who are already interested in what you offer. The best way to fail at business is to try and sell people on your ideas. They just don't care. Instead, you have to find out what people are looking for and provide it for them. This way, you are directing traffic instead of trying to create traffic.

There are tons of ways for you to generate leads, but I'm going to go about this from the perspective of someone who doesn't have a lot of money. I'm going to assume that you're just starting out, and you don't have a big budget to run ads and to do all sorts of marketing stuff. Keep in mind that this is a business we're talking about, and some money is required.

Let's recall the types of traffic that are out there. There's the traffic you control, like your email list. Then, there's the traffic you borrow, like paid ad traffic from Google or Facebook. Finally, there's the traffic you don't control, like traffic from the search engines and viral traffic from social media.

Whether or not you have a website, you will need a landing page where people can see your offer and give you their email. Clickfunnels is great for this. That landing page helps you acquire more of the traffic that you control. In other words, you want to grow your email list with as many qualified leads as you can. This allows you to send emails with offers to your subscribers and know that a certain percentage of them will buy what you are offering.

Clickfunnels isn't the cheapest solution out there, but it is one of the best. It is easy to use, and has an active user community. If you prefer a more affordable option and are willing to do more technical stuff, Thrive Themes is another good option that costs less, but you will pay with more of your time.

Now you have a landing page, and you're able to collect email addresses in exchange for your lead magnet. Once they give you that info, that person becomes a lead (aka subscriber). You now have permission to contact them by email. For businesses, I recommend asking for their phone number as well. It lowers your conversion rate, but right now, 90% of text messages are read, and that is powerful for getting your offer in front of people.

Once you have their info, you can add them to your email series. An email series is a set number of emails that provide the reader with insights and proof that you understand their problem and have the expertise to solve it. This helps to build their trust in you. This is vital because people rarely buy from someone they don't trust.

Whether it's a series of videos, articles, or podcast episodes, the point is that they hear you discussing their problem and demonstrating that you understand it and know how to fix it.

Let's get this out of the way. There is no better way to generate traffic than paid traffic. Email subscribers are great, but when you're just starting out, that's usually not a resource you have at your disposal.

Search engine traffic to your blog can work if you have the discipline to be consistent and the patience to wait for months before your traffic starts to trickle in. That also requires that you create long-form high-quality content. We'll discuss that later in this chapter.

So, if you don't have the advantages of an email list or popular blog, paid traffic is a great resource. However, paid traffic means spending money, and there is still a learning curve before you get good at it and make it worthwhile. Not to mention, paid ads can be costly, especially when you don't know what you're doing.

That's where video ads come in. I always recommend people who don't have a lot of money run video ads on YouTube. You can also run video ads on Facebook, but YouTube is a much better value in my opinion. You can literally run $1 a day video ad campaigns and get a bunch of people to see your video. All you have to do is demonstrate your expertise and how you can help them in a short video.

As of this writing in (July 2020), LinkedIn has geared their algorithm towards a preference for video. That is a good place to share your videos as well. If you can get your followers to view your videos on the day you release them and help them go viral. That costs nothing except the leg work to generate buzz within your LinkedIn network.

So, whether it's YouTube, LinkedIn, or Facebook (preferably all three), your audience gets exposed to your content, your expertise, and your call to action. Some of them will click and go to your landing page, which is a great way to generate traffic and leads.

Another way to generate traffic is to join niche relevant groups on Facebook and LinkedIn. Make sure that the groups have a couple of thousand members and that they are actively posting daily. You don't want to waste your time in dead groups. Then, engage in the groups for about 2-3 weeks so that people become familiar with your name and recognize you as a member of the group.

Find posts that ask questions that you can answer, and provide a quality answer to those questions, preferably with a Loom video. It doesn't have to be anything fancy. You don't even have to be on screen. You can make a video with an image of yourself and talk over the image. You make the video, post it in the group as an answer, and tell people if they have any other questions, they should DM (Direct Message) you.

When they reach out to you, and some definitely will, be helpful and then refer them to your landing page for more information. Make sure that you provide good quality answers to their questions so that their trust in you increases.

You'll notice that after a while, more group members will start hitting you up with questions. Don't stop adding value to the group. You want to stay top of mind. People have very short memories. By being consistent, you will ensure that you continue to get leads from the groups. They're going to send you direct messages. They're going to ask you questions. They're going to say, "Hey, can you help me with this?" That kind of stuff.

The way that you make yourself the most money is by providing people with the most value. They have to see you as someone that they know, like, and trust. Someone who is a guide, a consultant, a teacher. This will not only generate leads but, over time, will snowball, and you may want to start your own group.

Now multiply that goodwill that you generate in two or three Facebook groups and two or three LinkedIn groups. You jump on there, answer questions, for 10-15 minutes per group within an hour or so each day, and you've already answered a bunch of people's questions. Do 1 Loom video per day, and you'll have a bunch of people reaching out to you with more and more questions. This is great for you beyond generating business because when you teach, you learn, which increases your level of expertise.

The reason this is so powerful is called the rule of reciprocity. You will be generating all this goodwill by sharing your knowledge and time with people, and in return, you make the audience think, "this is someone I can trust." "Look at all that they do for the community for free." "Imagine what they'll do for me when I'm paying them as a client."

After you've been doing this for a couple of weeks, you're going to have a bunch of new friends. You're going to have a bunch of people who regularly ask you questions and start referring leads to you and things like that. This is lead generation at its best because it's organic. This is one of the best ways to generate leads without spending money.

But wait, there's more! It gets better because if you're answering questions on video in these groups, you can take those same videos, upload them onto YouTube, Facebook, LinkedIn, and Instagram and let people find you that way as well. In each video, you want to tell people, "leave me your questions in the comments so that I can answer them tomorrow because the content that I create is for you."

Then you make these quick three to five-minute videos answering one question each day. You title it. You put a couple of keywords in your description, add a link to your landing page as the first comment (YouTube doesn't like links in descriptions), and move on with your day.

Another way you can generate traffic is by creating high-quality blog posts from your videos' audio. I use a tool called Descript, and it transcribes 10 hours of video a month for $10 a month. That's pretty great! Now you're turning your videos into articles. You can take a couple of those articles, say your 10 best articles that get the most traffic, and turn those into an eBook.

You want to focus on making articles that are at least 2000 words. The reason being is that Google prefers articles that are at least 2000 words to rank on the first page of the search results. Those search results can bring lots of traffic over time. You just have to go into it, knowing that it's a long game strategy. The beauty of it is that each time you create one of those videos, it's also creating an article.

Here is another great way to get free traffic. Now that you have an e-book from 10 of your articles, you can use it as a lead magnet, or better yet, why not take 20-30 articles that you wrote while talking and answering questions for people and arrange them by topics and chapters.

If you don't know how to do this, you can pay somebody on Upwork or Fiverr to do it for you. After they're done formatting your articles into book form, you go to Amazon's CreateSpace and publish your book into an actual printed paperback book. Just like that, you are a published author.

You can add that to your resume and your LinkedIn profile. You can put it in all of your marketing, author, and coach – John Doe! Automatically you get credibility for being an expert. People are going to look at that and think, "this person has to know what they're talking about."

Because people always attribute expertise to people who write books, whether it's true or not. Many athletes and celebrities have best-selling books out, and many of those books are written by ghostwriters or biographers. That doesn't stop people from attributing expertise and higher status to these people. Those same principles will apply to you when you use them.

By being a published author, you can use the book to get onto podcasts. You can reach out to popular podcast hosts and say, "Hey, I'm an author. I'm coming out with a new book, and I'd love to be on your podcast." You hit up a bunch of these, and some of them will have you on their shows, exposing you to thousands of listeners. Some of them will look you up, join your email list, and buy your book!

Because you leveraged the attention of all of these podcasters' audiences, if you want to see how you promote a book, look up Chris Voss. Chris Voss is the author of a book called, Never Split the Difference. When his book came out, he was on every podcast known to man. I mean, he was killing the podcast circuit, and he was doing what he needed to do to make sure his book was a hit.

That's how you get your name out there. That's how you get people to purchase your book and join your email list. More than that, that's how you get people to come through and hire you as an expert, consultant, or coach. To me, that is one of the greatest ways to generate lots of traffic without really spending any money.

For those of you who have a more comfortable financial situation, I whole-heartedly recommend using paid ad traffic from Google and Facebook. Both for video ads and pay per click. Do keep in mind that both platforms, while similar, do require study and practice to master and get the best return on investment. Regardless of the ad budget, video ads are still my preference as people prefer video above all other forms of content.

Outsourcing

Earlier, we mentioned that you could have all of your business's technical tasks outsourced. So, this should come as a relief to you if you don't have a technical background. I'm going to show you some ways to get everything from the highly technical to the mundane done quickly and affordably.

First things first, to get things done efficiently in your business, you need to assess your strengths and weaknesses. For instance, if I had to start from scratch again, I would focus solely on these three things.

1. I would learn everything I could about copywriting. (Persuasive writing no to be confused with copyrights.)
2. I would learn all I could about email marketing. How to build lists, write great emails, engage the customer, and provide amazing value through engaging emails.
3. I would learn and master Pay Per Click Advertising (PPC), primarily Google Ads (that includes YouTube) and Facebook ads.

Regardless of whether you're just starting out or you've been doing this for years, this advice is well worth the price of this book. Because knowing and doing just those three things will cut out years of trial and error from your journey. If you only follow that piece of advice, you will thank me in the future.

Getting back to our assessment, you have to realize your strengths because as you begin to build your business, you're going to wear many hats, and there is so much to learn. Why waste time on things you don't enjoy or aren't good at. Experience has taught me that most of the things I learned I could have just outsourced and focused on the three skill sets I mentioned above (copywriting, email marketing, and PPC). This would have been so much better than spending countless hours learning everything under the sun since I'll never get that time back.

Add to that anything tech-related generally has an expiration date. So at least half of the tech you learn will have changed or disappeared within five years, but the skills that last for decades are the three I mentioned. Copywriting, email marketing, and Pay per click advertising have all been around for decades and are not going anywhere anytime soon.

They have additional advantages beyond longevity. They all make money, and only the ad platforms will change much. Copywriting and email marketing are about communicating with people, and ads that worked 100 years ago reworded a bit still work today.

Amateur entrepreneurs get caught up trying to learn new skill sets and soon find themselves overwhelmed, lose focus, become frustrated, and ultimately quit. This is why the myth that you can't make money online is so pervasive. Most people who tried didn't know how to or refused to outsource the tasks that were outside of their expertise.

This type of behavior leads to failure. When you're starting a business that you've dreamed up in your head, you're invested and passionate about the dream. That is until reality sets in; then, if you don't know how to overcome the obstacles, reality presents you more often than not, you will quit. The same thing happens offline with brick and mortar businesses, which is why 90% of new businesses fail, but nobody says offline business is a scam; go figure.

All this to say, do what you do best and pay others to do what they do best. For starters, I'm going to tell you about one of the best-kept secrets online. It's a site called Fiverr.com. It's a marketplace for outsourcers, and a lot of the jobs are done for just $5. I generally use Fiverr for professional voiceovers and quick graphic design jobs. Still, there is an endless amount of workers for all sorts of projects. The cover for this book was done by an artist I hired on Fiverr.

If you need a web programmer, researcher, SEO specialist, copywriting, or any number of higher-level services, there are quite a few good options available. My personal favorite is upwork.com. I've been using them for years, and I have nothing bad to say about them.

It takes time to read through the applicants, and my method for speeding that up is the 10-second rule. If I haven't seen something I like within 10 seconds of looking at their portfolio, I move on to the next applicant. It saves time, and it works wonders compared to when I used to look through the whole portfolio, hoping to find something I like.

Guru.com and Freelancer.com are competing services. I have heard good things about both, but I have never personally used them. If you can commit to the $200 to $600, it will cost for a decent part-timer. The best method by far is to hire a virtual assistant (VA) from the Philippines. This is my personal preference, 1 full-time VA from the Philippines is worth 2 to 3 full-time staffers from anywhere else, in my personal experience.

The work ethic, efficiency, and quality of employees you get from the Philippines far exceed what the dollar amount would lead you to believe you'll get. The site I use for this is onlinejobs.ph there you sign up, and view resumes, and contact the candidates to schedule interviews for just $69 a month (you can cancel anytime).

I usually communicate with candidates through Skype or Zoom and focus on their English as the hiring requirement. They are usually very capable and willing to learn whatever you ask them to. However, if their English isn't good, it probably won't result in a good experience for you or them.

If that all seems too involved, I recommend you go with a "done for you" service like VirtualStaffFinder.com. They have a network of qualified virtual assistants, and they vet them for you before you even start the interview process with the candidates they recommend.

Each of these sites has its own ins & outs that must be mastered. Still, they are viable solutions to your outsourcing needs. They should be more than enough to accomplish whatever tasks you need to be completed.

Conclusion

We've covered a lot of ground, and I realize that it can feel like you're drinking water from a fire hose, which is why I recommend going back and rereading some of the more complex concepts. I feel like most marketing topics aren't truly understood until you've gone over them a 3rd or 4th time. Don't give that a second thought; just do it. Repetition is an exercise for mastery. Then once you grasp it, go do it.

None of the words written on these pages matter if you don't put them into practice. I've taken courses from brilliant people, and without following through, the courses were worthless. Writing this book has been invigorating for numerous reasons, but one of the main ones is I am excited to see what you will build. I've compiled a list of tips and resources for you that have helped me in my own journey.

Do's

1. Take ACTION! Don't despair if, at first, you feel that you don't know what you're doing. Have no doubt that you will learn along the way. All travelers begin their journey once they leave home, not while they plan their trip.
2. Start imperfect and perfect along the way. Remember that "good is good enough." Don't wait until you're "ready," as that day may never come.

3. Ignore what you lack and focus on what you have.
4. Remember that you're playing a long game. You probably won't make a million dollars in your first month (if ever). Still, with patience, study, and persistence, you can build a successful business.
5. Always remember that done is better than perfect.

Don'ts

1. Most people quit, don't be one of the many.
2. Don't forget the important things in life, friends, and family and building good memories. Cherish them.
3. Remember that money brings comfort and possibilities, not happiness. Don't make the mistake of letting your income define you.
4. Don't let setbacks stop you. Failure is never permanent.
5. Never forget that your best customer is the one you have already. Always keep them coming back for more.
6. Finally, don't tell people what you're doing; tell them what you've done. Friends and family mean well, but they will discourage and criticize you more often than not.

Essential Reads

Below is a list of some of the books that have shaped my view on how to do business. They are rich both in knowledge and wisdom, but also insightful as to how and why people become successful.

They provide timeless pearls that will help you to see things that may have once seemed impossible as only small bumps on the road. I recommend that you pick them up and learn a wealth of valuable business knowledge. The financial benefits and satisfaction you acquire in this time investment will be well worth the sacrifice.

1. Napoleon Hill - Think and Grow Rich
2. George Clason - The Richest Man in Babylon
3. Dale Carnegie - How to Win Friends and Influence People
4. Og Mandino – The Greatest Salesman in the World
5. Robert Kiyosaki – Rich Dad Poor Dad
6. Chris Voss – Never Split the Difference

I could have added numerous classics to the above list, but I decided to keep it down to my most memorable ones. These are the books that left me thinking and talking about them long after I had read them. Do yourself a favor and read each one.

Resources

The following tools are what I recommend for doing business online.

Web Tools

- Gmail Account – It's a basic necessity when using Google services.
- Calendar App – It's said that 90% of success is just showing up.
- Google Drive – You need cloud storage, and it comes with Gmail.
- Google Analytics – Know your site's stats. GA makes it easy.
- Google AdSense – When you're just starting out, it's easy money.
- Loom – Makes screencasts a breeze, and it's free.
- LastPass – Remembers your passwords, so you don't have to.

Paid Business Accounts

- Aweber— My preferred email autoresponder for beginners.
- Bluehost – High value, low cost hosting at its best.
- Clickfunnels - The leader in marketing tools and super easy to use.

Essential Gear

- Blue Yeti Mic – Professional audio quality with USB plug and play.
- External Hard Drive - Archive your work and save yourself headaches.
- Headphones - The MEE Audio M6's are my headphones of choice.
- Mac or PC – If you want your work to be easier, get a Mac.
- Smartphone – Record videos in HD, upload to YouTube, and done.

Final Thoughts

Writing this book has been an incredible journey for me, and I'm glad I took it. I am confident that the skill set I've shared can be used to create a full-time income. With this information, you can build your own lead magnets, landing pages, affiliate sites, and ecommerce stores. You can create a membership site, do coaching and consulting, or build WordPress sites for clients. You can do these things yourself or hire freelancers to do them for you. The possibilities are endless... It's up to you and your imagination; all you have to do is start and remember that consistency is the key.

It is my sincere hope that you will not talk yourself out of believing these truths but instead believe in your ability to persevere and figure it out until you have realized your dreams.

I would love to hear about your results; connect with me here:

Facebook - https://www.facebook.com/groups/abovebeyonders
Podcast - Above & Beyond Podcast with Ark Pizarro
Website – https://arkpizarro.com

If you found this book helpful, please leave a review and share it with a friend or two.

Thanks!

Now, go build something great!

Glossary

Ad Network - A company that connects advertisers to websites that want to host advertisements.

AdSense - A program run by Google where website publishers in the Google Ad Network serve text, images, video, or interactive media advertisements

Advertiser - A person or company that advertises a product, service, or event.

Affiliate Marketing - Performance-based marketing in which a business rewards one or more affiliates for each visitor or customer brought by the affiliate's own marketing efforts.

Campaign - An organized course of action to promote and sell a product or service.

Clickbank - Global internet retailer and affiliate marketplace.

Clickfunnels - A sales funnel builder designed to help businesses automate their sales processes.

Click-Through Rate (CTR) - The ratio of users who click on a specific link to the number of total users who view a page, email, or advertisement.

Copywriting - Copy refers to the output of copywriters, who write material that encourages consumers to buy goods or services.

Domain Name - A unique name that is used to identify and direct traffic to a website.

Email Autoresponder - Email marketing tools that immediately provide information to their prospective customers and then follow up with them at preset time intervals.

Fiverr - An online marketplace for freelance services.

Google Ads - An online advertising platform developed by Google, where advertisers pay to display brief advertisements.

Google Analytics - A web analytics service offered by Google that tracks and reports website traffic.

Hosting - A type of Internet hosting service that allows individuals and organizations to make their website accessible via the World Wide Web.

Keyword - A term used in digital marketing to describe a word or a group of words used to perform a search in a search engine.

Landing Page - A web page that appears in response to clicking on a search engine result, marketing email, or an online advertisement to capture website visitors' information in exchange for branded content.

Lead Generation - Lead generation initiates consumer interest or inquiry into a business's products or services.

Lifetime Value (LTV) - Lifetime value predicts the net profit attributed to the customer's entire future relationship.

List Building - List building is growing your email list by collecting people's email addresses.

Niche - A specific area of marketing which has its own particular requirements, customers, and products.

Outsourcing - To procure goods or services needed by a business from outside sources and/or suppliers.

Pareto's Principle – Pareto's principle states that, for many events, roughly 80% of the effects come from 20% of the causes.

Pay Per Click (PPC) - An internet advertising model used to drive traffic to websites, in which an advertiser pays a publisher when the ad is clicked.

Plugins - A software component that adds a specific feature to an existing computer program.

Publisher - A person or company that displays ads on their digital space. They connect users with advertisements.

Return on Investment (ROI) - A ratio between net profit and the cost of investment. A high ROI means the investment's gains compare favorably to its cost.

Screencast - A digital recording of computer screen output, also known as a video screen capture or a screen recording.

Search Engine Optimization (SEO) - The process of growing the quality and quantity of website traffic by increasing the visibility of a website or a web page to users of a search engine.

Search Engine Results Page (SERP) - Web pages served to users when searching for something online using a search engine, such as Google.

Server - A computer program or a device that provides functionality for other applications or devices, called "clients."

Shopify - Shopify is a commerce platform that allows anyone to set up an online store and sell their products.

Subscriber - An internet user who permits a particular brand to send regular emails to them.

Theme - A collection of templates used to define the appearance and display of a WordPress or Shopify website.

Thrive Themes - WordPress site builder designed to make your entire website convert more of your visitors into subscribers.

Website Traffic - The amount of data sent and received by visitors to a website. This is determined by the number of visitors and the number of pages they visit.

Transcription - To make a copy of dictated or recorded matter in longhand or with software such as audio to text apps.

Upwork - A global freelancing platform where businesses or individuals connect to conduct business.

URL - The address of a World Wide Web page.

Virtual Assistant - A virtual assistant is generally self-employed and provides professional administrative, technical, or creative assistance to clients remotely.

WordPress - A free content management system used to build and maintain websites.

About the Author

Ark Pizarro is an accomplished digital marketer, author, and host of the Above & Beyond Podcast. He is known for creating highly profitable marketing campaigns that dramatically increase sales and brand loyalty instead of the overpriced mediocrity of typical marketing agencies.

Ark helps people win at entrepreneurship through coaching in digital marketing, personal finance, investing, and real estate. His goal is to help 1000 people build six-figure businesses.

Ark Pizarro lives in Dallas, TX, with his wife and four children.

ADVANCING POSSIBILITIES

www.ingramcontent.com/pod-product-compliance
Lightning Source LLC
Chambersburg PA
CBHW032013190326
41520CB00007B/451